GOD,

SNATCH

MY

FEAR!

30 Prayers to Overcome Fear

Nicci the Great, LLC

God, Snatch My Fear

Also, by Nicci Gardner

Figurines Dancing in my Head

The Spirit Within: Understanding the Holy Spirit for the Novice

Nicci Gardner

God, Snatch My Fear: 30 Prayers to Overcome Fear

Publishers' note: This book is not intended as a substitute for critical or spiritual professional counseling. It should not be treated as such.

ISBN: 978-0-578-99509-0

DEDICATION

I dedicate this book to my best friend, God. Thank you for your love, support, generosity, and protection. Thank you for being so interactive with me and giving me creativity beyond measure. Thank you for opening my blind eyes. Thank you for being my saving grace and my hiding place. Thank you for never giving up on me, even when I gave up on myself at times. Thank you for giving me everything that I didn't know I could possibly need. Thank you for knowing me better than anybody else does. Thank you for being the God of the gap and filling all the voids. I could go on endlessly about how much I appreciate your very existence. No words in any language here on Earth can fully articulate how much I adore you. In this dedication, I offer this book to you as a token of my undying love.

CONTENTS

PREFACE

Prayer of Introduction

Lord,

We want to begin with acknowledging the blessings you have showered down unto us...the food, clothes, answered prayers, health, and protection you have provided. We are aware of all that you do for us to which we have not yet even been exposed. In this, we lift you up and bless you for your mercy, grace, and substance.

Second, we ask you to forgive us for what we have done to offend you and your word. We ask you to separate us from all unrighteousness and put a divide between us and sin as far as the East is from the West, including even the sins we are not aware of committing. Please forgive our unknown sins.

We ask you to be with those we encounter. Allow us to reflect you and your character. Grant us the power to pour into them according to their need.

In this book, we are coming together in agreement, asking that you, God, snatch away all our fears. Not some, but ALL! Replace those fears with wholehearted confidence in you.

Nicci Gardner

"GOD,

SNATCH

MY

FEAR"

30 Prayers to Overcome Fear

ONE

Fear from the past...

1. A Prayer that Hashes Out the Past

Lord,

My past haunts me like a bad dream on repeat. I can't seem to get through one day without thinking about how unfair my life was. I've spent countless years enduring the emotional hardships of my past. I don't want to be afraid of anything that reminds me of an old scenario or situation. I want to look towards my future with open-mindedness and complete faith in you. Oh, Lord, in this prayer, I do, for the very last time, hash out the old memories, feelings, and events. I release the people who hurt me. I release the decisions that were made on my behalf. I ask you, God, to take away the emotional tie that has me bound to the past. I am asking you to replace it with a strong connection to you and your infinite love for me. In Jesus' name, Amen.

2. A Prayer Relinquishing the Strong Emotional Connection to the Past

Lord,

The emotional attachment I have to the past weighs me down like an anchor. Every journey, season, and new chapter I enter, I drag this rotten bag with me. It keeps me negative and depressed. It drowns out my accomplishments and prohibits me from experiencing true praise and worship with you. God, allow this prayer to be a prayer of deliverance from my connection to the emotional turmoil of my past. My past is my history, not my emotional bondage. In your name, snip the tie that binds me. In Jesus' name, Amen.

3. A Prayer that Accepts the Past

Lord,

I accept the past as my history. I will not hide, run, or deny that from which you have delivered me. Help me to understand that my past is behind me. Help me to consider that as a closed chapter and assist me in receiving the abundance of blessings through another door. In Jesus' name, Amen.

4. A Prayer against Mental Replays

Lord,

I've heard people refer to you as the great healer. In this, God, I am asking you to stop the mental replays of my past. The anguish that hits my mind and soul during these tormenting thoughts is abusive to my life. I give these images to you. The unhealed areas of my mind, I give them as well. The characters in the plays, I release to you. In your holy and beloved name, I do declare a complete stop to the traumatic events that plague my processing. Lord, I leave these at your feet. In Jesus' name, Amen.

Nicci Gardner

5. A Prayer that Forgives the Past

Lord,

Forgiveness is easier said than done. I know that I cannot forgive without you. Lord, I am asking you to help me want to forgive. My flesh wants to hang onto the trespasses people have committed in my life. When I choose to hang on to the offenses, it locks me into the other person's actions, behaviors, and decisions. In this, unforgiveness prohibits my own personal growth in you. I want to forgive my enemies. Lord, grant me a forgiving heart that fully releases people from my heart. Teach me to love, understand, and see people the way you do. In Jesus' name, Amen.

6. A Prayer that Releases the Past

Lord,

Any other components that have me in partnership with my past, I release them all to you. I give you my everything; you are everything and I need. Help me to walk in the abundance of you and all your creation. In Jesus' name, Amen.

Nicci Gardner

7. A Prayer of Thanksgiving to God for a Healed and Closed Chapter

Lord,

I spend so much time asking for things. In this prayer, I just want to thank you. Thank you for seeing the depths of my heart. Thank you for seeing me the way nobody else does...for seeing past my outside and influencing me the way you do. Thank you for your abundant healing powers that I needed ever so much. Thank you for showing me what I buried in pain and sorrow. Thank you for shifting my internal atmosphere and allowing me to let go of the past in peace. Because of you, my great counselor, I can finally close a chapter of my life. Again, thank you. In Jesus' name, Amen.

TWO

Fear of the future…

8. Prayer against Fear of the Unknown

Lord,

I know I can be myself with you. I don't have to portray a false reality or act a certain way to make you feel differently about me. I can be real. I know that you would see right through it if I did. In honesty, I fear the unknown. I worry about what is there and who is there. I don't want to see my past in my future. I do not want any repeats. God, I humbly ask you to remove the fear of my future and replace it with a confidence in you and not in myself or anyone else. Help me to hear your voice clearer, even if I am in the dark. Lord, I will follow you anywhere, even into the unknown. I rebuke any fear of the unknown in your precious and holy name. Allow me to fully stand in the unknown without fear, but in faith. In Jesus' name, Amen.

9. Prayer Accepting the future

Lord,

The future looks like a scary place at times, especially for a person who is changing their mindset on life; and I want to focus on the cup being half full, not half empty. I know that seeing the future prematurely is not what I need. In this prayer, I am accepting my future in you. Whatever it brings, I will walk in your righteousness and perfect will for my life. I relinquish my future to you, and I fully accept the contents in it. I trust that you will provide, protect, and minister to me. In Jesus' name, Amen.

Nicci Gardner

10. Prayer to Fulfill My Purpose

Lord,

I long to be obedient to you. I want to do what you have created me to do. Distractions are ever upon me, and I venture off course easily. I pray to you for focus. I need to totally focus on you and your will. I know without a shadow of a doubt you have a purpose for me for which you specifically designed me. Lord, I want to fulfill that purpose for your kingdom. Give me the tools I need to be successful in the purpose. Give me your divine power to enable me to thrive in that purpose. Lord, I rebuke all principalities that are aimed at destroying me and my purpose. Lord, in you, I am more than enough to complete the assignments you have given me. Help me as I run this race; bind all my fears associated with my purpose and allow me fulfillment in Jesus' name, Amen.

Nicci Gardner

11. Prayer to Conquer Fear of a Faith Walk

Lord,

I know that for my relationship with you to grow, I must trust you. In trusting you, I must listen to your divine guidance. To be guided, I must move. I like to refer to this ideology as walking in the dark or faith walking. Faith walking is scary for me sometimes. The first few steps are the most nerve-wracking. I want to do more walking with you. I don't want to be scared while I do it either. I know I must depend on you for survival, assurance, and support in this walk. I feel you waiting on me. With my eyes closed, I grab your hand. Taking deep breaths, I am trusting you as you lead me in this journey. I. Will. Trust. You. In Jesus' name, Amen.

12. Prayer Releasing Generational Curses

Lord,

I pray for you to break all chains that bind me, including generational curses and witchcraft that may be attached to me and my bloodline. By me accepting you and your blood that was shed on Calvary, I tear down any strongholds in my genes—financial, sexual, mental, physical, emotional, spiritual, and any other tie of my forebears that holds me in yesterday; I pray for complete release and atonement. I want to be liberated to worship you in wholeness and deliverance. God, free me from the fear of walking in the curses that plagued my ancestors. Lord, release me from generational curses in Jesus' name, Amen.

13. Prayer for Contentment

Lord,

I want to be happy. I need to be earnestly, honestly, and purely content with myself and life. I don't want to feel a gap or empty space. Allow me to experience peace with where I live, what I eat, what I wear, what I drive, and free me from competing with others and their possessions. I want to be happy with what you have given me and not lacking. God, I know that the fear of me assuming I don't have what others have robs me of my joy and will not allow me to be whole in you. Lord, I decree contentment in my life and in my home. In Jesus' name, Amen.

God, Snatch My Fear

THREE

Borrowed fears...

14. Prayer against Imagined Fear

Lord,

My imagination can play some foolish tricks on me at times. Constantly thinking about how many ways things can go wrong and the failures associated with that makes my mindset negative. Negative thinking is a faith killer in the first degree. I don't want to be pessimistic, but I want to be optimistic. Any new venue you present before me, I want to receive it in prosperity and thankfulness. Lord, remove not just some, but all, of my imagined fears. I need to be set free from the fear of my imagination. In Jesus' name, Amen.

Nicci Gardner

15. Loss of My Fantasy World

Lord,

When my stress levels are high, I retreat mentally to fantasy worlds in my head. I created them as a pre-teen, and I have lived in these fantasies long enough. They are not of you. I want you to be my permanent hiding place. I am scared to lose these fantasies, even as odd as I think it is to mention a fear of losing them. They have brough me so much artificial pleasure. As I contemplate their contents, none of it is surrounded by you or your glory. They make my mind drift to things that are demonic and not of you. The life I have chosen to live revolves solely around you. Thank you for bringing this to my attention. I need my face always attached to your feet, even if it hurts. I am heartbroken to even say this prayer, but I know it must be done...Lord, kill my fantasy worlds. I want you to be my only hiding place. In Jesus' name, Amen.

16. Prayers Against Others' Fears for Me

Lord,

I don't want other peoples' fears to be extended to me. Their fears are not mine, and I refuse to be haunted by them. I have my own individual relationship with you, and I am fully leaning on your promises. God don't allow me to associate the fears of someone else with my own life and what you have for me. In this, Lord, I rebuke all fear that attempts or has infiltrated my perception of you and what you have for me. Free me from other people and their fear. In Jesus' name, Amen.

17. Prayers against Principalities and Darkness

Lord,

You remind us in your Word that the enemy is seeking to sift us as wheat. I do not want to have a fear of the darkness or what entities lurk in its shadows. Allow me to remember that fear is not of you. In your holy and precious name, we bind all principalities and darkness that has contacted us or looms over us to make contact. Any unclean spirits in or around my life, I ask you to choke them out like yesterday's laundry! You have given me your Holy Spirit, and we can rebuke all unclean spirits by that power. In Jesus' name, Amen.

18. Prayer for a Sound Mind

Lord,

Frustration, anxiety, and emotional instability infect my mental processing. I am asking you for a consistent soundness of you in my mind. I don't want to my relationship with you to be scarce and sporadic. I pray for complete healing from any mental health issues: bipolar disorder, clinical depression, suicidal ideas, schizophrenia, borderline personality, multiple personality, psychosis, substance abuse, eating disorder, post-traumatic stress, obsessive-compulsiveness, or mood disorders. I ask you for restoration of my mind and divine protection of the portals of my mind. Lord, ANY fear that looms in the crevices of my mind, I ask you to stomp it out and replace it with everything concerning you. In Jesus' name, Amen.

19. Prayer to Live and Thrive

Lord,

I want to walk in the fullness that you have for me. I want to be successful and live the life you have for me. I rebuke the fear and spirit associated with poverty. Allow me to walk in substance and increase. I don't want to fear my needs not being met. I want to live without a fear of not having what I need for tomorrow. I pray that I grow, have enough to share, and that I thrive in life fearlessly. In Jesus' name, Amen.

FOUR

Fear of failure...

20. Prayer for Wisdom and Knowledge

Lord,

Ignorance does not look good on me, let alone on anyone else. In this, I am afraid of failure for my lack of knowledge and wisdom. I am scared that some individual or a group of people will take advantage of my ignorance, and that I will fail as a result. I am also nervous about walking in the purpose you have for me because I feel as though I am not qualified or educated enough. Lord, forgive me for partnering with fear. In your holy Word, you promise that *"if any of us lack wisdom, let us ask of God, that giveth to all men liberally, and upbraided not; and it shall be given him. But let him ask in faith, not wavering."* Allow me to stand confidently upon your Word. Eradicate my unbelief. I know that you qualify the called; you do not call the qualified. In you, I am complete, and fear is not of you. I am growing in faith daily, and I treasure my relationship with you. I rebuke the spirit of failure in the name of Jesus, Amen.

21. Prayer for Strength During Constructive Criticism

Lord,

I know you chastise those whom you love. Every time I make a mistake or do something goofy that is not in alignment with your word, I struggle to forgive myself. You are more forgiving of me than I am of myself. In a twisted way, I want you to punish me harshly and pull your spirit from me. But you never do. Instead, you pull me closer and encourage me to repent. You also comfort me and remind me that you aren't going anywhere, and nothing can separate me from you. Lord, help me not to fear making mistakes bad enough to affect my relationship with you, causing me to feel as

Nicci Gardner

though I am not good enough for you to correct. Thank you for loving me through my ups and downs. I pray I get closer to you every day. In Jesus' name, Amen.

22. Prayer to Release Ourselves Wholeheartedly and Completely (Submission)

Lord,

I want to release my mind to you completely. I do not want to hold back anything. I also do not want to return to old processing. I want to make decisions by asking you for guidance. I fear that I drift to old things that brought me pleasure, things that are against your will for me. In this prayer, I am relinquishing full ownership of my deepest thoughts and desires. I want to control my mind, and I bind the unclean spirit of drifting or wandering in my thoughts. I pray that I focus on you, your Word, and the assignments you have given to me. In Jesus' name, Amen.

23. Prayer against Being Too Hard on Ourselves

Lord,

I fear not being good enough. In this prayer, I stand on the incredible value I have in you, based on the great investment you made not only for me, but for mankind. I pray against me rejecting myself. Allow me to see me the way that you see me, which will also help me to see others the way you see them. I rebuke the spirit of tormenting critique. I thank you for loving me in a way that shows me how to love others. I no longer will be so hard on myself that it separates my mind from focusing on you. In Jesus' name, Amen.

FIVE

Fear of our own Value...

24. Prayer Accepting Our Own Value

Lord,

I struggle with esteem and confidence at times. I find myself wrestling with the fear of not being good enough, smart enough, spiritual enough, and even loveable enough to be accepted by you. I know this toxic notion is from the enemy.

He knows that if I think lowly of myself, I will engage in things that are beneath me and your statues. God, I accept my value in you. No longer will I entertain any more negative perceptions of myself. I have great value in you. You sent your only son to the world as a sacrifice to save us and, when you did, you were thinking of me. Allow me to walk in the love you have for me. In Jesus' name, Amen.

25. Prayer against Rejection

Lord,

I fear rejection, not just from myself but from others, and especially in my purpose. I cannot harbor the spirit of rejection; it will consume my success and affect my worship. I trust you fully, and others' behaviors or decisions on how they receive me is none of my business. I will not internalize any negative feedback, neither will I regard rejection as a representation of me. In you, I am complete, and I know that every day I am growing In you. In Jesus' name, Amen.

26. Prayer against Abandonment

Lord,

Fear of abandonment is a wicked beast. You can't fear this unless you have already experienced it. Sometimes being abandoned is the best thing that could happen to us, whether it is temporary or permanent. Lord, I now know that in the heat of abandonment is when we are exposed to you and your presence the most. I want to say thank you for the abandonment I experienced, as crazy as it sounds. If that person had not abandoned me, I would not be so close to you now. Their absence left a gap wide open that left me searching. The search led to me finding you, and you are the God of the gap. Thank you for fulfilling me in ways that no one else could. In Jesus' name, Amen.

27. Prayer for Power to Fast

Lord,

I know I would benefit greatly from fasting.... not just sporadically, but regularly. I know this sounds a little corny, but I get scared during fasting. The hunger pangs make me feel like I'm starving, and it makes me extra emotional. Lord, give me the power I need to fast and not fear the side effects. I know fasting can break strongholds, give clarity, and help me to hear you better. In Jesus' name, Amen.

28. Fear of Relationships

Lord,

I have a ridiculous fear of new people getting close to me. I know that I have some emotional scarring from past relationships with friends, family, and lovers. The intense fear that I feel when someone wants to connect with me past being acquaintances is debilitating. Out of all my fears, this one is probably the most crippling. To be bluntly honest, I want to keep this fear. In a weird way, this fear makes me feel safe; if I keep this fear, it serves as a great barrier or wall from anyone else hurting me. In retrospect, this decision is toxic, and it locks me out of receiving love from the people that you send to me. God, assist me with wanting to let go of this fear. Loosen my grip from it and ease my mind. I need to focus on all the things I will miss out on and not the things that could go wrong in new relationships with people. Lord, snatch my fear of relationships with people. In Jesus' name, Amen.

29. Fear of End Times

Lord,

I cannot even lie; the news scares me. Ever since the beginning of the first quarantine, my biggest fear of doomsday at hand troubles me. You clearly state in your word about the end times and what to expect, but I still get nervous. Becoming sick from covid, losing a close loved one, the wars, the weather acting crazy, you name it—it all makes me very uncomfortable. In this prayer, I am asking you for a peace during the storm. I want to be so wrapped up in you and have so much confidence in your edge of protection that these events do not phase me in the least. Whatever coverage I am faced with, I pray for a calmness in my spirit that surpasses all understanding. I want my faith to be unwavering. In Jesus' name, Amen.

30. Prayer of Forgiveness for Partnership with Fear

Lord,

Forgive me for partnering with fear. Fear is not of you, and you speak against this multiple times in the Scriptures. In this, we have given you all our fears...a collection of our past and present. We leave them at your feet and pick them up again no more. From this moment on, we are new creatures. Free from ill thinking and making decisions from broken places. We are now whole and solid in our faith in you. Use us and purge us from anything that might have slipped our minds. We are your vessels to be used to grow your Kingdom. Thank you for your forgiveness. In Jesus' name, Amen.

www.ingramcontent.com/pod-product-compliance
Lightning Source LLC
LaVergne TN
LVHW012340100826
845148LV00018B/3219

* 9 7 8 0 5 7 8 9 9 5 0 9 0 *